HOW TO

KINDNESS

The Inculcation Of Empathy,
Compassion, Feelings, Tolerance And
Good Virtues In Children

COPYRIGHT

All rights reserved. No part of this book may be reproduced, distributed, or transmitted in any form or by any means, including photocopying, recording, or other electronic or mechanical methods, without the prior written permission of the author, except in the case of brief quotations embodied in critical reviews and specific other non-commercial uses permitted by copyright law. For permission requests, write to the author, addressed "Attention: Permissions to copy," at the address below.

EMAIL:
BELLASTARDOM101@GMAIL.COM

DEDICATION

I specially dedicate this book to all children worldwide.

TABLE OF CONTENTS

TITLE PAGE — i

COPYRIGHT — ii

DEDICATION — iii

TABLE OF CONTENTS — iv

CHAPTER ONE

Kindness As A Good Virtue — 1

CHAPTER TWO

Understanding Children's Emotional Model — 6

Why Your Child/Children Needs More Kindness — 10

CHAPTER THREE

Different Approaches You Can Use In Teaching Your Kids How To Be Kind — 13

CHAPTER FOUR

Fun Games And Activities To Teach Kindness	39
Box Of Good Deeds	40
Love Pyramid	43
Group Circle	45
Kindness Jar	47
Emotional Check	49

CHAPTER FIVE

Kindness Workbook Questions	51
OTHER BOOKS BY THE AUTHOR	53
CONTACT THE AUTHOR	56
NOTES	57

CHAPTER ONE

KINDNESS AS A GOOD VIRTUE

Kindness works together with empathy and compassion, so they are all interwoven into good virtues. Showing empathy is the imagination of how someone or others are feeling in a particular situation, and the ability to respond with utmost care. It is so complex a skill to develop because it requires some special approach and processes.

Kindness may mean doing certain things or might take a different approach according to the individual's perspective and cultural background. For little kids, kindness might mean waving to an elderly neighbor, sharing snacks with a younger sibling, or singing a lullaby to make a crying baby fall asleep. And for older kids, it might mean comforting a sad or scared person, accompanying a friend on an errand, or donating some of their pocket money for a cause they love.

Whatever the act of kindness means to you, it is important to help in nurturing the virtue in your children right from their tender age

Nurturing and raising a child who is empathic to others should be the joy of every parent. A child who really cares about how his or her behaviors affect others is generally a child with good virtues. A child like this will feel remorseful and a deep streak of empathy runs through his or her mind whenever he or she made a mistake and works hard to correct it.

However, parents cannot prevent a child from feeling angry, hurt, disappointed or sad; because these are common and normal human emotions. But when a parent is emotionally in tune with the child when he or she is going through these emotions, it gives the child the impression that he or she isn't alone and also fosters closeness between the child and the parent. Therefore, a child who constantly receives empathy will have the ability to regulate his or her emotions healthily. And this helps him or her in having empathy for others.

CHAPTER TWO

UNDERSTANDING CHILDREN'S EMOTIONAL MODEL

As discussed earlier, either you are a parent, teacher, or caregiver; one of the greatest and mind relieving hope is to see that your kids are kind and good to people. Whenever they have a chance to help others, you hope they will and never turns to be intolerant, wicked or prejudiced.

But on a serious note, it's not that easy to be kind to others, even for us as a parent. Why? Because trying to help others might seems difficult when we feel like we don't even have the help we needed ourselves.

One important thing to note is that; kindness can be learned just like any other behavior through a repetitive process. And most of the ways children learn new behaviors are by copying from those around them, which gives us adults a challenging opportunity and responsibility to teach and lead by example.

This is because, during childhood, kids' brains are naturally wired with mirror neuron cells which allow easy imitation of behaviors around them. So, when kids notice an action, their brains instantly respond as if they are actually performing the action themselves. At this stage, the kids' brains are easily moldable because they have less time to solidify lifelong behaviors.

WHY YOUR CHILD/CHILDREN NEEDS MORE KINDNESS

As we can see nowadays, judging others has become a norm practiced by many people all around the world. People find it very easy to make comments about other people whether they are celebrities or regular citizens, this behavior is not a new one because it has been since time immemorial. So, the speed, anonymity, and ease at which people post different comments and pass judgments on others are so alarming. The children who are monitoring the tech and social media are learning from what they see around them. This exposure to toxic, wicked and bullying habits they see online will definitely affect how they treat other kids. Naturally, kids are self-centered which means they don't always put themselves in other people's shoes or think logically about how others might feel, though this does not mean that kids are naturally unkind. Kids are wired to have empathy for other people and may want to help them. So as a parent, teacher, caregiver; you can just take advantage of these natural habits and encourage your kids to practice kindness in their daily lives.

CHAPTER THREE

DIFFERENT APPROACHES YOU CAN USE IN TEACHING YOUR KIDS HOW TO BE KIND

PUT THEM IN OTHER PEOPLES SHOE

It is important to remind children to put themselves in other people's shoes before they take any action. You can ask your child to think deeply before saying something about someone, and to take time to consider how he or she might feel if the same thing is said about him or her by others. How would he or she feel if she found out that someone was making jest of the way he or she talks, or if he or she is being criticized for being slow in writing? Would he or she like someone encouraging him or her for trying or castigating him or her for not performing well? Also, would he or she wants someone to praise him or her for doing something or would he or she want someone to make fun of him or her? Using these strategies will mold your kids in having empathy for others and show them how to be kind to others.

USAGE OF THE WORD THANK YOU, PLEASE, AND SORRY

Teaching children good etiquettes such as greeting people properly, politely talking to people, showing respect to others is an integral part of raising a good and kind child. And in as much as you are living with your children at home, you will definitely reap the rewards of raising and having kind and nice individuals growing up in your home.

GO AGAINST ONLINE AND OFFLINE BULLYING

As a parent, you should be aware of the dangers of bullying, either physical bullying or cyber-bullying. Therefore it is important to monitor your children's activities and how they treat other children, you should also be vigilant about what your children see and read online, it's also crucial to monitor what he or she is writing and sharing on social media.

TEACHING HIM OR HER TO SAY NICE THINGS

Teach your kids how to say positive things only, that is; the type of things that people will make them feel good and happy rather than being sad. It is equally important like an adage that says: "it's better to keep quiet than saying something that will get others depressed". Teach him or her how to hold his or her tongue whenever he has a negative opinion about something. For instance, if a friend asks him or her if he or she likes a painting that he or she made, and he or she didn't like it, he or she can say something nice about it instead of using negativity to kill the friend's morale. Nice words such as "the colors you used are nice" or "I like this concept" or other nice compliments are the best way to go, he or she shouldn't say what he or she didn't like about it.

AVOID SPOILING YOUR KIDS

It is good to take care of our children and give them the best things of life they deserve but you cannot buy everything they want for them, as a parent you should let them understand why they can't get everything and should know the reasons why they can't get everything they want. Therefore you need to teach them the concept of being patient, charitable, and thankful and having self-control. To teach them all these successfully, you must make sure you don't spoil them by exercising restraints in giving them anything they ask every time.

ASK YOUR KIDS TO SEND KIND THOUGHT TO OTHERS

Teaching your children the acts of kindness can come in the form of wishing for the well-being of others. Sometimes you can ask your kids to imagine someone who might be going through some difficult issues, and they would like to send their kind thoughts to and should say it loud and clear.

Something like "It will be well with them", "I wish them happiness" etc. This kind of practice helps children to think about kind thoughts every time.

TEACH THEM RANDOM ACTS OF KINDNESS

You can practice random acts of kindness; to the extent, they may not even know who did it. This random act can be anything that will make others day a little brighter. You can also instruct them to perform the random act for their sibling(s), neighbor(s) or teachers at school, or any other person you think might be applicable.

VOLUNTEER FOR OTHERS

Teaching children acts of kindness requires living by example; there are several ways to lend a helping hand, either through helping other people or helping animals.

Therefore, involving your children in volunteering is a good way to teach them how it feels good to be helpful. You can volunteer by cleaning your street, picking garbage from the park, helping the aged to cross the road, wheeling the disabled and other acts of kindness. With these habits, this will grow the acts of kindness and helping others in your kids, and they will pick all or some of the acts of kindness displayed.

The good thing about being kind to others is that it makes us feel good and takes away the attention off our problems, creates a feeling of fulfillment. So, this is why it's important to raise a kind child who will use the act of kindness to lift himself and others around him or her, this will, in turn, help him or her to become a loving and happy person.

BE PATIENT WITH YOUR KIDS AS THEY LEARN

To effectively teach your kids the acts of kindness, it requires some bit of patience from your side as a parent. Everything is level by level because your child wouldn't be perfectly empathetic by age three, even some teenagers haven't even mastered being empathetic completely, it is a complex skill that requires gradual process and will continue to develop later across your kid's life.

EXPOSE THEM TO REALITY OF LIFE

To effectively teach your kids the acts of kindness, sometimes it is necessary to let them face the reality of life and see how other children who are unprivileged like them are living. There are numerous children in the world who have low or no food to eat not to talk about owning a toy. Talking about this moral issue will make them have compassion for the less privileged and treat others with kindness.

DISCUSS WHAT EVERYONE IS FEELING AFTER CONFLICT

The best time to discuss feelings is after a conflict, that is when the kids are separated and have calmed down, then ask and discuss what each of them was feeling previously. Trying to discuss feelings when the kids are having conflict will make things more complicated. Younger children can be guided just to figure out what they have been thinking and feeling at that time of the conflict.

OBSERVE YOUR KIDS FROM A DISTANCE

The most effective way to truly know your child's personality is through observation. By paying close attention and watching how he or she relates to others is an excellent way to tailor your responses and reactions to him or her. From the observations you made, it will be easier for you to correct or encourage him or her on how best to treat others kindly.

SHARE STORIES OF EMPATHY

Share books and stories that bother on kindness and empathy themes. There are a lot of great stories and books to choose from, and research has shown that telling stories is a powerful and influential way of inculcating knowledge in children without direct teaching.

For younger children, read out stories loudly that will invoke their imaginations, while for older children, you should stock their reading list with empathy and kindness filled storybooks.

TEACH THEM HOW TO READ PEOPLES EMOTION

Kids need to learn how to read people's emotions face-to-face, so try to enforce the rule of the talker's eye to help them use facial expressions, voice tone, eye contact, and emotional cues in determining how others are feeling.

READ AND WATCH TV TOGETHER

This is another way to teach your children empathy. When watching a movie or reading a book together, make sure you focus on characters that apply to kindness, from there; discuss the character and their behaviors as the story progresses. TV shows like **Daniel**

Tiger is an example of a TV show that teaches kindness and empathy, and this will work perfectly when you and your kids discuss what is happening as you are watching it.

LET THEM SEE HOW YOU RESOLVE CONFLICT WITH OTHERS

While it is almost impossible to avoid arguments or conflict in front of kids, it is equally important to know that if children didn't see conflict resolution in your relationship, it will be harder for them to be able to resolve conflicts later in life in their relationships. The best thing to do after a conflict or argument with your partner is to make sure you resolve it in front of the kids. This will model them into someone who has empathy and feelings for others, and this will teach them how to resolve conflicts with other people.

IMPORTANT THINGS YOUR KIDS NEEDS TO KNOW ABOUT KINDNESS

The following are what your children need to know for them to have empathy for others:

Understand that he or she is a separate individual

Understand that other people can have a contrasting opinion against his or hers.

Be able to notice the common feelings other people experience such as surprise, sadness, anger, joy, disappointments, etc.

Be able to observe a particular situation and imagine how he or she or the person will be feeling at that moment.

Be able to imagine the best and appropriate response in comforting someone who has a problem

CHAPTER FOUR

FUN GAMES AND ACTIVITIES TO TEACH KINDNESS

Note: *Although most of these games and activities are suitable for a group of children, you can practice it with a single kid too, just that you will make some minor adjustments to the instructions.*

BOX OF GOOD DEEDS

Study shows that reminding children of their past good deeds is a way of encouraging positive thoughts and ability to help and treat other people with kindness.

The box of good deeds is a fun activity that can be tried with children of almost any age.

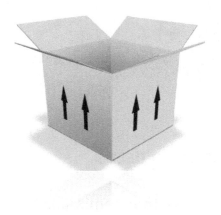

Get a carton or box, instructs each kid to turn to one of their neighbors and tell him or her something good, then they should write the good thing on a sheet of cut-out small circles or hearts of paper.

They should write as much as possible the good deeds they can remember with the name of the beneficiary on it and put it in the carton or box.

After they are done, open the carton or box and read out loudly the good deeds of everyone as written in the papers. This can also be done with only one kid, just tell him or her to remember the good deeds he or she has got from others, write it out with their names or any identification tag and drop it in the box of good deeds.

This activity of sharing their good deeds will definitely put them in a positive mood, and sharing of others' good deeds will make them feel loved and affirmed by others.

LOVE PYRAMID

This is a good and great game for triggering positive emotions, try to remember what you and your kids love together. There will be among your kids that love pets; some may love toys, some playing video games while some may love watching TV and so on. Just make sure the kids build the love pyramid themselves, start from the eldest one by having him or her name what he or she loves most, the eldest should place his or her hand in the center, then the children say what they love and places their hand above the eldest child's own, this way you have created a love pyramid.

GROUP CIRCLE

This is another activity that encourages unity and teaches children the act of kindness.

To start this activity you need to create a group of the kids circularly and choose an object as the talking piece, this can be a microphone, mobile phone, small beach ball, etc. The talking piece will be passed around the group, and you should notify the kids that anyone who currently holds it has an exclusive speaking right and others must keep quiet and listen attentively while he or she is talking.

Introduce a topic or ask a question from that you would like them to respond to, after invoking the conversation, take your seat in the circle and become a member too instead of a leader. The group circle is good in helping the kids relate with one another, and this will encourage them to share and accept feelings that might prove difficult for them to talk about.

KINDNESS JAR

This activity is carried out to encourage the act of kindness, and the best way to do it is through creating a kindness jar.

Start by writing down the names of various good deeds on pieces of paper, something like; "say thank you to a friend", "say I love you to a friend", "hug your neighbor", "play together with a friend", and any other good thing you can think of, then put the notes in a jar. So allow the kids to randomly draw the notes in the jar and do whatever is in the note picked. With the practice of this activity, happiness and kindness will be inculcated in the mind of the kids.

EMOTIONAL CHECK

This is among the simplest activities of kindness but it has a higher potential to encourage a good emotional state.

To use the emotional check, you can trigger a question like; "how are you feeling today?" This will make the children acknowledge that we are all humans and our feelings and emotions change day to day, thereby making them less paranoid whenever they are feeling negative.

After asking the question, you can instruct the kids to turn and talk to their neighbor and ask the same question from him or her. With this activity, you will be able to get the students to be in their right frame of mind and be more kind to the other; also this will help you in identifying potential problems with a specific child.

CHAPTER FIVE

KINDNESS WORKBOOK QUESTIONS

What do you understand by kindness?

Where do emotions come from?

Describe a moment when you felt empathy towards someone, either you are happy or sad because you can sense what **he/she/they is/are** feeling?

Give a rough estimate of the number of people you have shown kindness to this year so far

What are the ways you are might plan to work on to expand your empathy by showing care and concern for others?

What will you do if someone needed your help but you are not capable to render it?

What have you learnt from helping others?

How do you feel in your mind when you help others?

When will you apply the skills you have learned here?

OTHER BOOKS BY THE AUTHOR

You can also get these books written by me (Bella Stardom) which are:

TEACHING CHILDREN HOW TO RESPECT PERSONAL SPACE.

It is available in both Kindle and Paperback, kindly click on the image or the links below to grab a copy.

Kindle:

https://www.amazon.com/dp/B07ZZ95R17

Paperback:

https://www.amazon.com/dp/1705462871

ANGER MANAGEMENT FOR KIDS WITH ANGER ISSUES

Kindle:

https://www.amazon.com/dp/B0828HF81N

Paperback:

https://www.amazon.com/dp/1670899292

CONTACT THE AUTHOR

For any enquiries, suggestions, feedbacks and any other information; you can contact the author by email at BELLASTARDOM101@GMAIL.COM

NOTES

Made in the USA
Columbia, SC
04 December 2023